Production-Ready Microservices on Google Cloud

A Definitive Handbook

By Navveen Balani

Production-Ready Microservices on Google Cloud

A Definitive Handbook

By Navveen Balani

Copyright @ 2019 by Navveen Balani. (http://navveenbalani.dev)

All rights reserved. No part of this publication may be reproduced, distributed, or transmitted in any form or by any means, including photocopying, printing, recording, or other electronic or mechanical methods, without the prior written permission of the publisher.

All other trademarks or registered trademarks are the property of their respective owners.

July 2019: First edition

Although the author and publisher have made every effort to ensure that the information in this book was correct at press time, the author and publisher do not assume and hereby disclaim any liability to any party for any loss, damage, or disruption caused by errors or omissions, whether such errors or omissions result from negligence, accident, or any other cause. Use of the information and instructions contained in this work is at your own risk.

Introduction

Containers are becoming a standard way to run and scale microservices across multiple cloud providers. With Kubernetes, the job of deployment, scaling, and management of containerized applications on cloud or on promises is now mainstream and extremely streamlined.

To build a production grade environment, however, you need a host of other components like Virtual Private Network (VPN), endpoint management for microservices, load balancer to balance request over various protocols (HTTP, HTTP(s), Web socket), Configuring SSL, Health monitoring of services, Network configuration like Whitelisting of IPs, Network address translation (NAT) for Outbound connections, and ensuring logging at various entry points in the application.

In this book, I will go through the steps to create a production-ready environment on Google cloud for deploying microservices. The book follows a step by step tutorial approach and the steps outlined are generic and can be applied to build your production topology on similar lines.

The book assumes you are familiar with Kubernetes and Google cloud. The book introduces some of the concepts briefly while setting up the production environment and deploying the solution.

This book is part of our "The Definitive handbook" series. Our vision in the – "The Definitive handbook" series is to enable our readers to understand the technology in simple terms and provide a go-to reference and a recipe for building any real-world application using the latest technology.

This is our fourth – "Definitive handbook" series work, the first being – "Enterprise IoT" (https://amzn.to/2LrLfGm) which got acknowledged as one of the Top Computing book for 2016 by computingreview.com (http://computingreviews.com/recommend/bestof/notableitems.cfm?bestYear=2016). The second series book was "Enterprise Blockchain" (https://amzn.to/32AbDTK) and third one was "Real AI" (https://amzn.to/32w1UOx).

For any comments, suggestions or queries, please reach me at
me@navvenbalani.com

Table of Contents

CHAPTER 1. BUILDING THE ENVIRONMENT 1
   ENVIRONMENT AND SOLUTION OVERVIEW 1
   HIGH-LEVEL STEPS 2
      Solution 1 - Using Google Ingress Controller 2
      Solution 2 - Using Nginx Ingress Controller 3

BUILDING THE SOLUTION 1 - USING GOOGLE INGRESS CONTROLLER
.... 4
   CREATE THE VPN 4
   CREATE A PRIVATE INSTANCE OF GOOGLE KUBERNETES CLUSTER 7
   CREATE CLOUD NAT CONFIGURATION 13
   DOWNLOAD THE MICROSERVICE APPLICATION AND DEPLOYMENT SCRIPTS FROM
   GITHUB 18
   BUILD THE MICROSERVICE CONTAINER 20
   PUSH THE MICROSERVICE CONTAINER TO THE GOOGLE CONTAINER REGISTRY
   21
   DEPLOY ENDPOINT FOR THE APPLICATION 23
   CREATE WORKLOAD, SERVICE AND INGRESS 25
   INVOKE THE MICROSERVICES 35
   CONFIGURE CLOUD ARMOR 36
   TEST THE MICROSERVICES WITH CLOUD ARMOR 40

BUILDING THE SOLUTION 2 - USING NGINX INGRESS CONTROLLER
.... 43
   INSTALL NGINX INGRESS 44
   CREATE WORKLOAD, SERVICE AND INGRESS 49

MONITORING THE SERVERS 57
   WHAT'S NEXT 59

SUMMARY 60

Chapter 1. Building the Environment

Containers are becoming a standard way to run and scale microservices across multiple cloud providers. With Kubernetes, the job of deployment, scaling, and management of containerized applications on cloud or on promises is now mainstream and extremely streamlined.

To build a production grade environment, however, you need a host of other components like Virtual Private Network (VPN), endpoint management for microservices, load balancer to balance request over various protocols (HTTP, HTTP(s), Web socket), Configuring SSL, Health monitoring of services, Network configuration like Whitelisting of IPs, Network address translation (NAT) for Outbound connections, and ensuring logging at various entry points in your application.

In this chapter, I will go through the high-level steps to create a production ready environment on Google cloud for deploying microservices. The steps outlined are generic and can be applied to build your production topology on similar lines.

Environment and Solution Overview

We would be deploying a set of microservices (as containers) on Google Kubernetes Cluster. We would use Google Endpoints for API management and deploy the google endpoint container along with our microservices container.

We would further create an Ingress Controller (of type Load Balancer) and expose our application microservices over HTTPS. All incoming HTTPS requests would go to a Load balancer, which would direct them to one of the nodes in the Kubernetes Cluster. In the nodes, the requests would first go to Google endpoint (which would validate the endpoint key and logs all endpoint request) and then to the respective microservice endpoints.

There are additional requirements on ensuring only authorized IPs access our microservices. We will learn how to whitelist the IPs using two approaches - Google Cloud Armor and Nginx Ingress Controller (instead of the default Google Ingress Controller).

Similarly, for outbound connections, we would be connecting to third-party services. The third-party services employ similar IP whitelisting requirements, and we'll need to provide our set of outbound IPs that would connect to these third-party services. For this requirement, we would be use Google Cloud NAT to provide our private Google Kubernetes Engine (GKE) clusters the ability to connect to the Internet, as well as Static outbound IPs that we can configure and provide to third-party services to whitelist on their servers.

High-Level Steps

The following are the high-level steps that we would carry out to build and deploy our microservices configuration. It is assumed that the Google project is already created.

Solution 1 - Using Google Ingress Controller

1. Create a VPN
2. Create a private instance of Google Kubernetes Cluster.

3. Create Cloud NAT configuration.
4. Download the microservice application and deployment scripts from GitHub.
5. Build the microservice container.
6. Push the microservice container to the google container registry.
7. Deploy endpoint for the project.
8. Create Workload, Service, and Ingress (GCE ingress).
9. Invoke the microservice.
10. Configure Cloud Armor.
11. Test the microservices with Cloud Armor.

Solution 2 - Using Nginx Ingress Controller

The Solution 1 above uses default Google Ingress Controller. We can also use Nginx Ingress Controller as it provides a lot of add-on features like IP whitelisting, rule configuration, HTTP(s) redirect etc. The deployment process is the same as described in Solution 1, except for Point 7 and Point 8. For Point 7, we would install Nginx ingress first on our Kubernetes Cluster and then deploy the Nginx Ingress configuration for our application (instead of GCE ingress). We don't need Cloud Armor as the whitelisting of IPs is supported through Nginx Ingress directly.

In the next chapter, we would go about building the solution.

Building the Solution 1 - Using Google Ingress Controller

In this chapter we would go about building the production topology and deploying our microservices application using Google Ingress Controller

Create the VPN

The first step is to create a virtual private network for our solution.

Go to Networking -> VPC Networks - > VPC Network - > Create VPC Network.

We will create a custom subnet in us-east1 region and specify the IP address range so that it is large enough to accommodate our network. For instance, Kubernetes cluster would assign each node a range of IP addresses from the IP address range specified, so that each Pod can have a unique IP address. To know more about how to size the cluster, please check out the Considerations for Cluster Sizing section at https://cloud.google.com/kubernetes-engine/docs/how-to/alias-ips.

The following is a snapshot of the VPC network that we created for our application. You can use a similar configuration based on your network topology. The below IP address range configuration is large enough to suffice for most networks.

Figure 1 - VPC Network Configuration

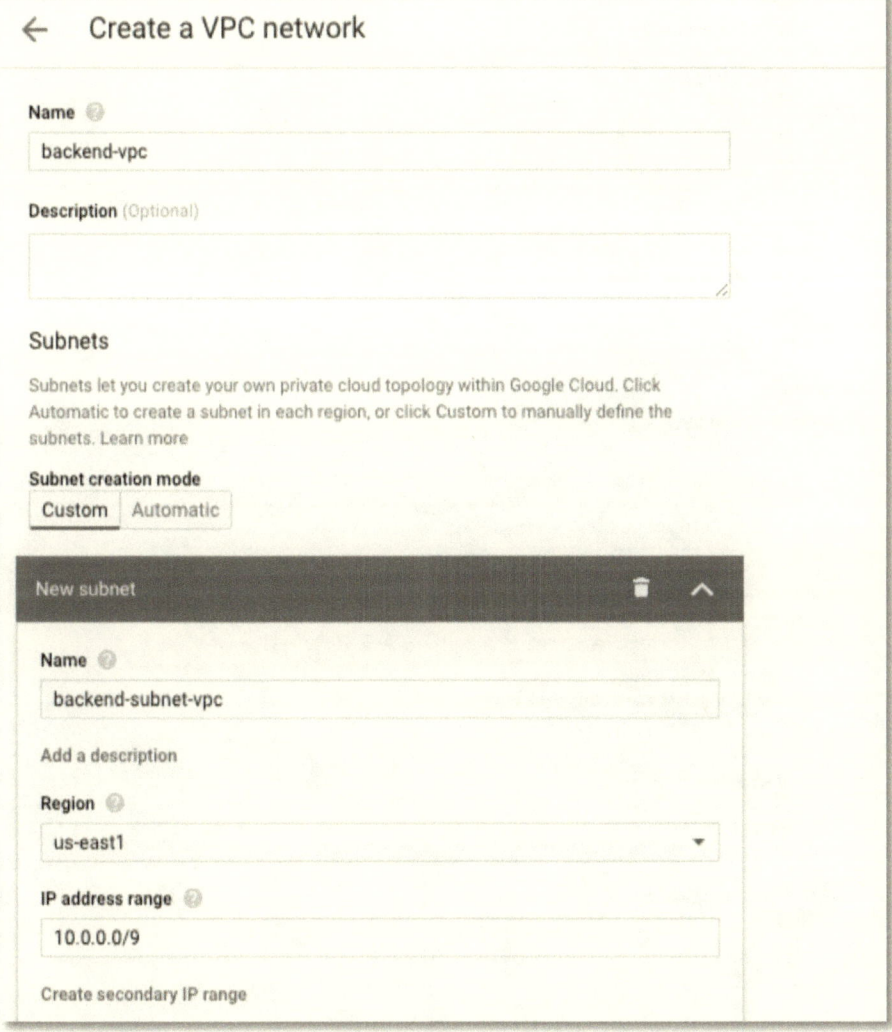

Figure 2 - VPC Network Configuration - Additional Settings

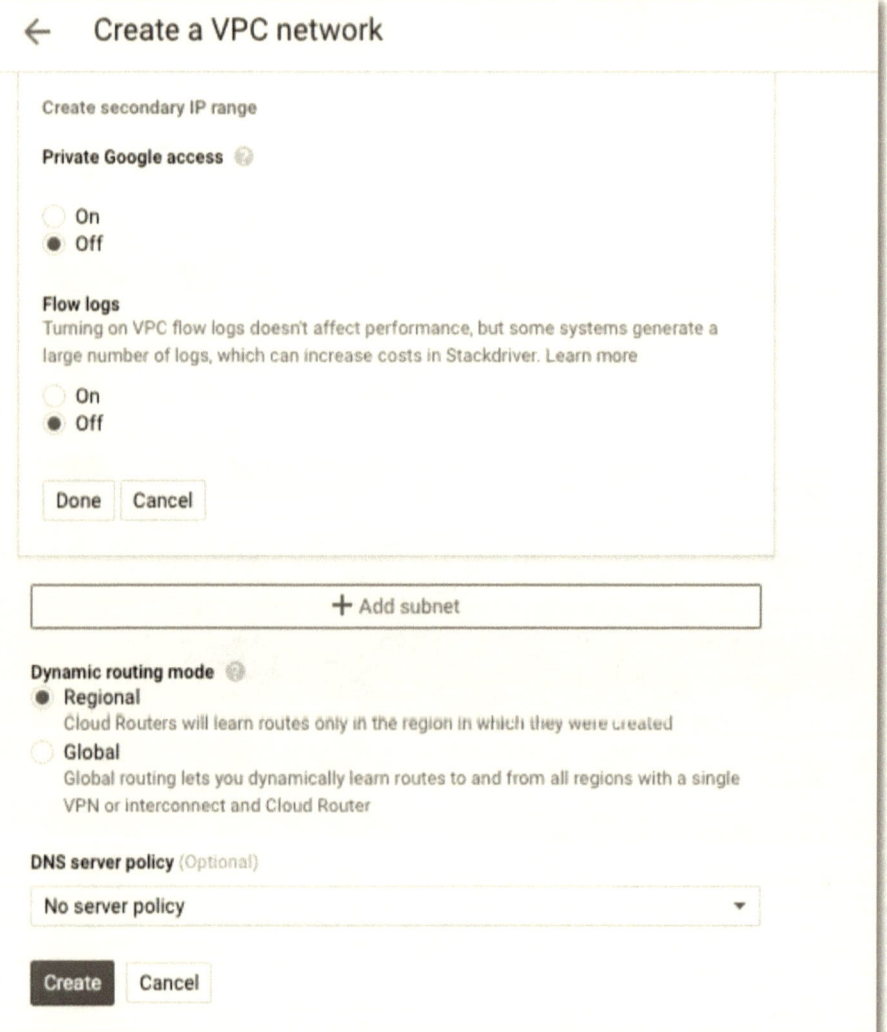

Create a Private Instance of Google Kubernetes Cluster.

Next, we would create a private Google Kubernetes Cluster (GKE). A private cluster ensures that all nodes and the master server (every cluster has a Kubernetes API server called the master) are isolated from the public Internet. You can configure which IPs have access to the master.
You can also set up a Load Balancer that accepts public traffic and directs it to the cluster. For more details, please refer to https://cloud.google.com/kubernetes-engine/docs/how-to/private-clusters.

Go to Kubernetes Cluster - > Clusters - > Create Cluster.

Follow the steps below to create the cluster.

- Create a Standard cluster. Provide the name of the cluster and zone as us-east1-b (i.e. that should be part of the VPN region). The VPN that we created earlier was in the us-east1 region. We can also create a Regional cluster.

Figure 3 - Cluster Configuration

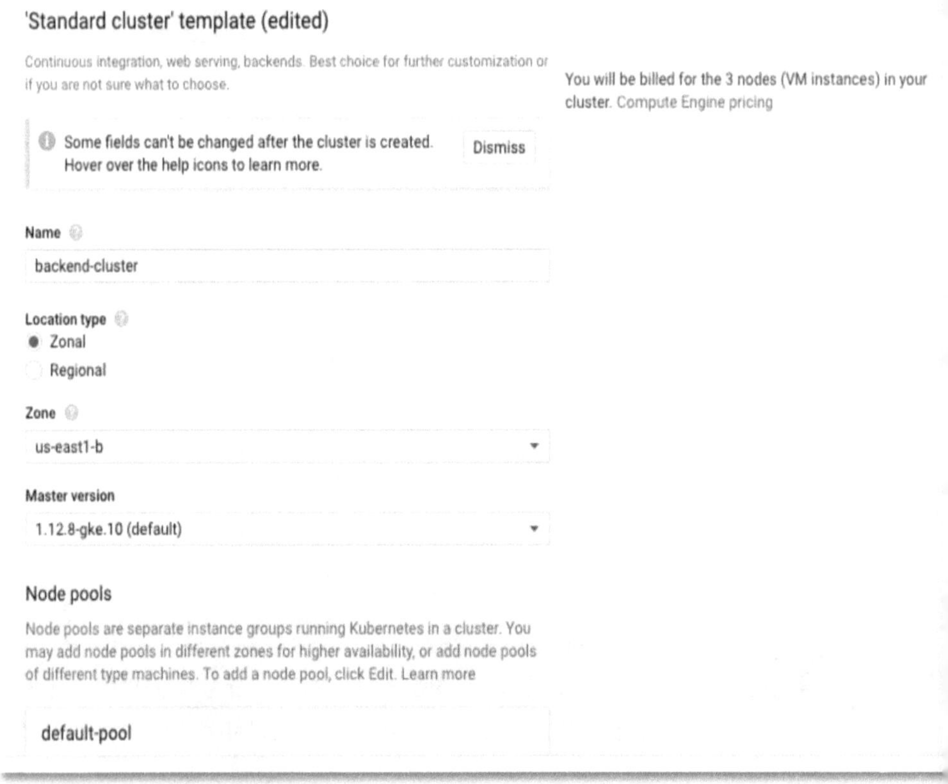

'Standard cluster' template (edited)

Continuous integration, web serving, backends. Best choice for further customization or if you are not sure what to choose.

You will be billed for the 3 nodes (VM instances) in your cluster. Compute Engine pricing

ⓘ Some fields can't be changed after the cluster is created. Hover over the help icons to learn more.   Dismiss

Name
backend-cluster

Location type
● Zonal
○ Regional

Zone
us-east1-b

Master version
1.12.8-gke.10 (default)

Node pools

Node pools are separate instance groups running Kubernetes in a cluster. You may add node pools in different zones for higher availability, or add node pools of different type machines. To add a node pool, click Edit. Learn more

default-pool

- Enter the number of nodes as 3 and the machine type based on your workloads. For our sample microservices application, a small machine type is good enough. 3 nodes should be good enough to start with since our cluster will auto scale based on workloads.

Figure 4 - Cluster Configuration – Node pools

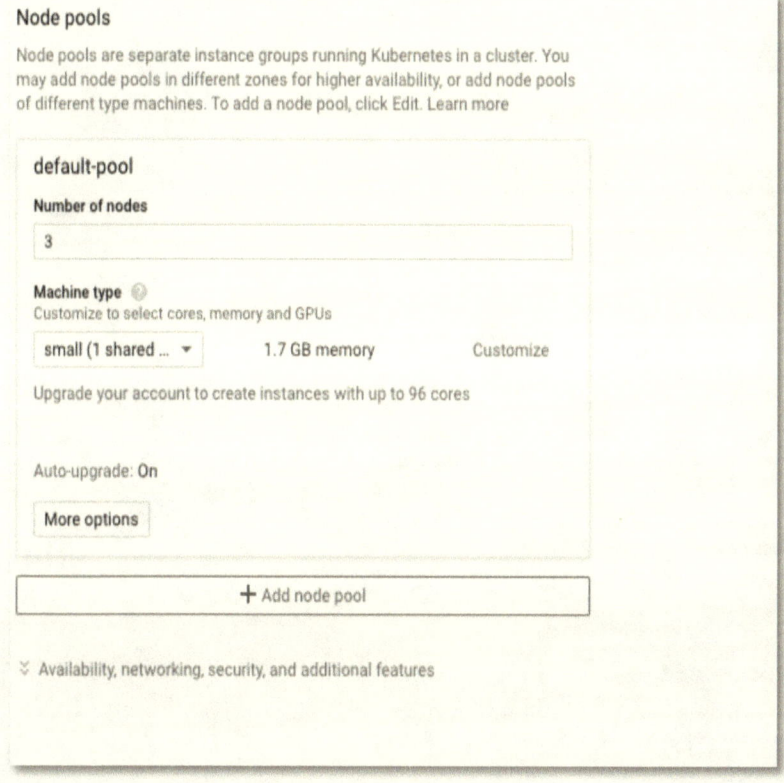

- Click Enable-VPC native and select the VPN network and subnet that was created earlier in Step 1.

Figure 5 - Cluster Configuration – Networking options

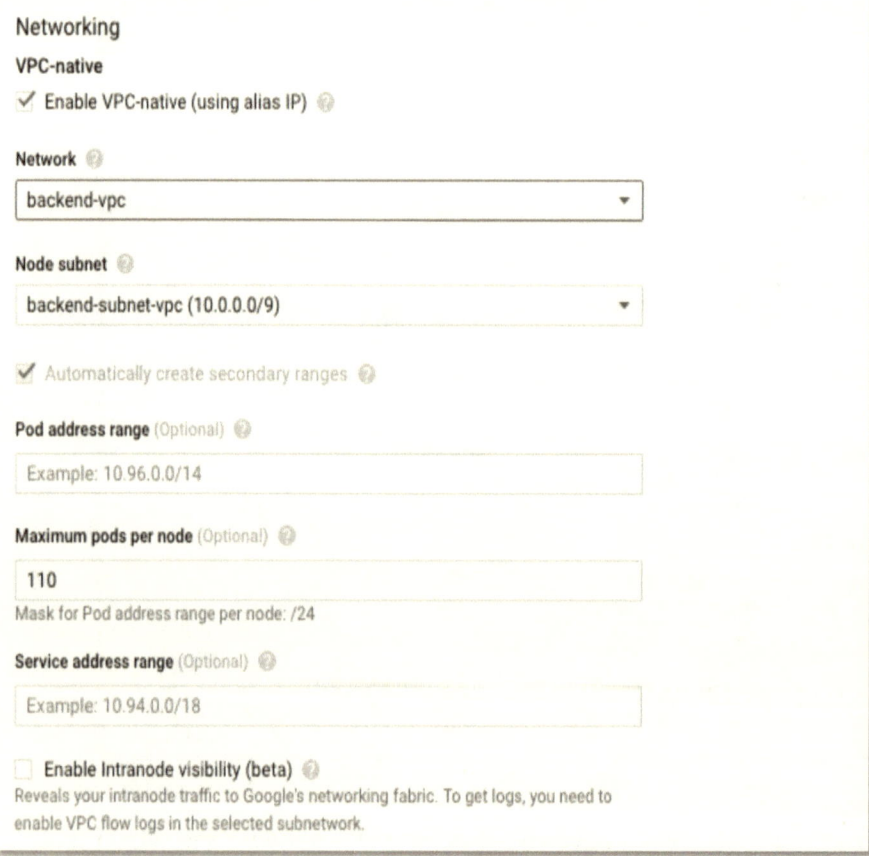

- Select Enable Http Load balancing for the load balancing component. Select Private Cluster and Select Access Master using its external IP address and specify the IP address. Click Enable master authorized networks and specify the IP which can connect the master. We specify 0.0.0.0/0 for now to allow access from any IP address for running the deployment scripts (or you can create a VM in the same VPN network and connect to the master). Please remove the authorized network once the deployment is done.

Figure 6 - Cluster Configuration – Security options

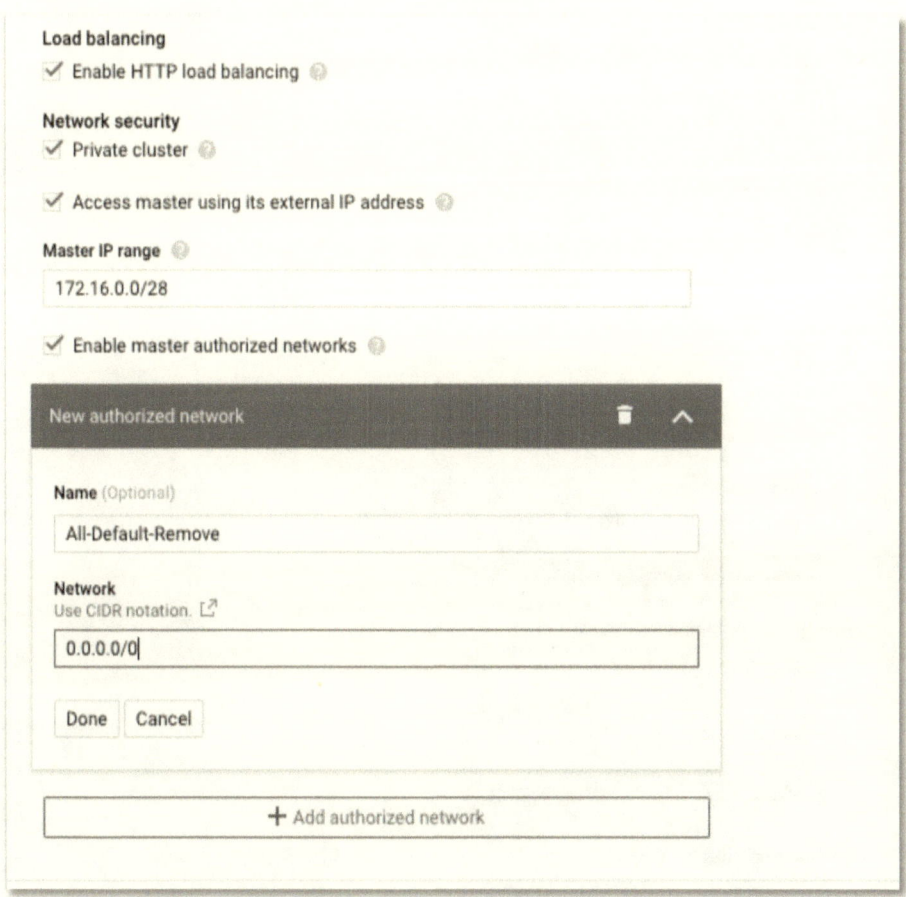

- o Next, enable the logging features and create the cluster.

Figure 7 - Cluster Configuration – Logging options

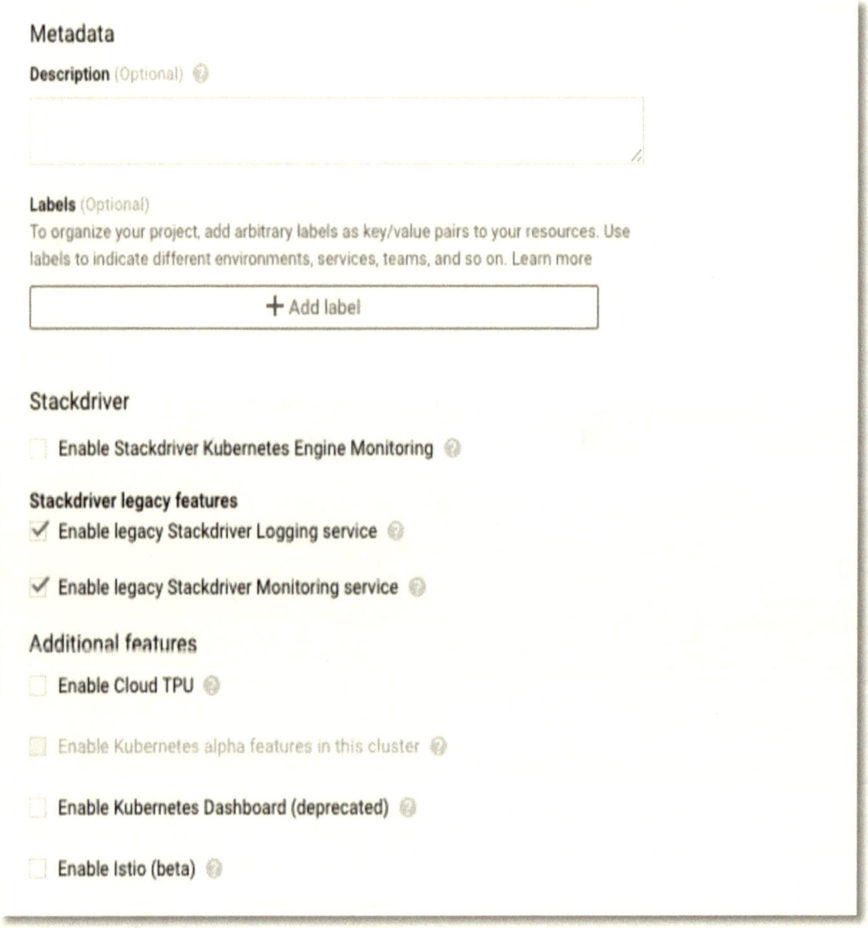

Metadata

Description (Optional)

Labels (Optional)
To organize your project, add arbitrary labels as key/value pairs to your resources. Use labels to indicate different environments, services, teams, and so on. Learn more

➕ Add label

Stackdriver

☐ Enable Stackdriver Kubernetes Engine Monitoring

Stackdriver legacy features

☑ Enable legacy Stackdriver Logging service

☑ Enable legacy Stackdriver Monitoring service

Additional features

☐ Enable Cloud TPU

☐ Enable Kubernetes alpha features in this cluster

☐ Enable Kubernetes Dashboard (deprecated)

☐ Enable Istio (beta)

Create Cloud NAT Configuration

In this step, we would create Cloud NAT. Cloud NAT allows VMs instances without external IP addresses and private Google Kubernetes Engine (GKE) clusters to connect to the Internet.

Cloud NAT implements outbound NAT (i.e. network translation, mapping internal IP addresses to external IP) to allow instances to reach the Internet.

Go to Network Services - > Cloud NAT - > Create NAT Gateway
- Enter a name for gateway and select VPC network as backend-vpc (created in Step 1).
- Select the region as us-east 1 (same as the VPC region).

Figure 8 – Create NAT Gateway

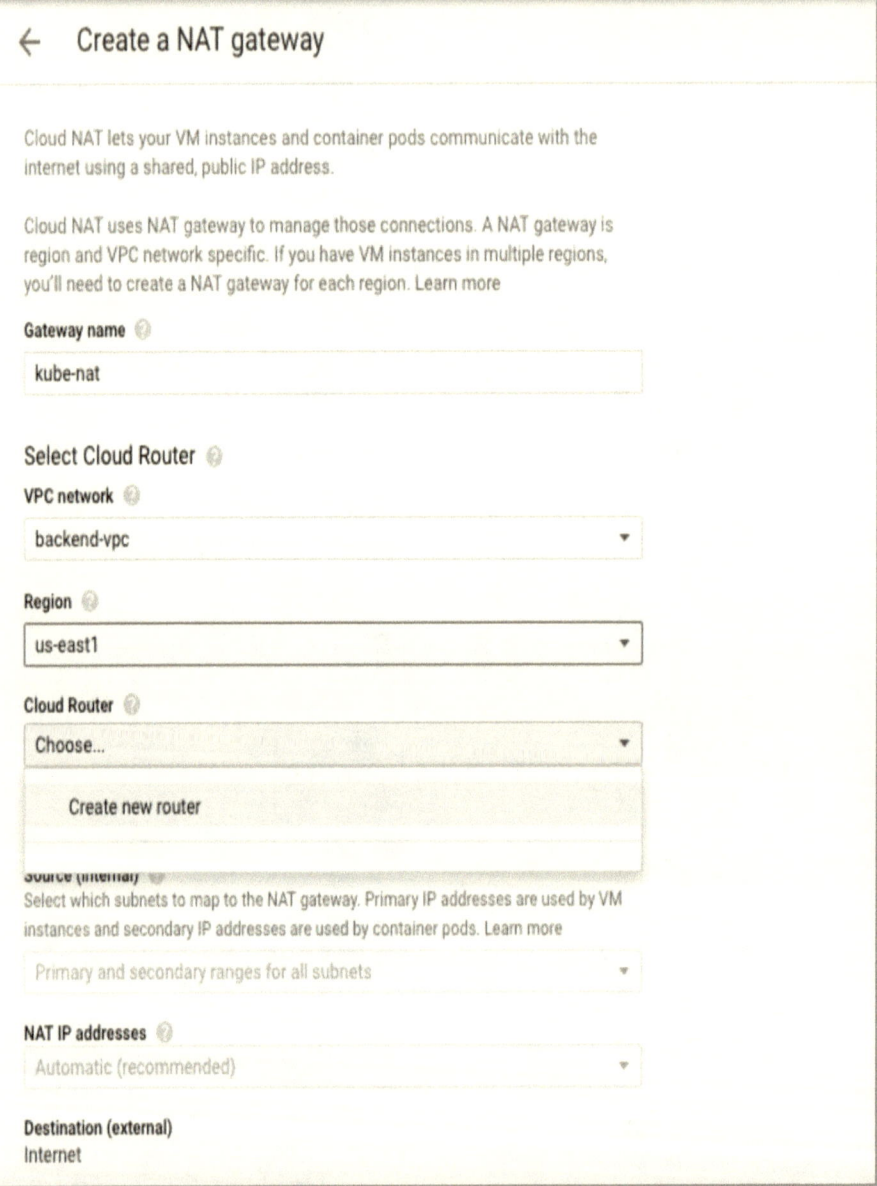

- Click create new Cloud router. Enter the name and click continue. Cloud Router enables dynamic routing for the VPC. For more details, kindly refer to https://cloud.google.com/router/docs/concepts/overview.

Figure 9 – Create Router

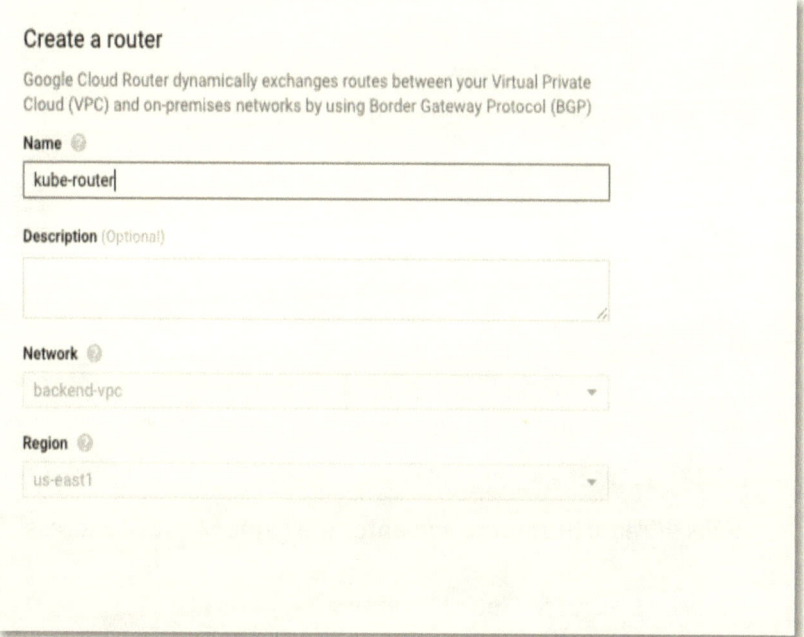

- In the NAT mapping, select Manual NAT IP address. We don't select automatic as we would like to reserve a set of IPs that we can provide to external services/partners to whitelist on their servers. Choosing automatic would create and release IP based on workloads.

Figure 10 – Create NAT Mapping

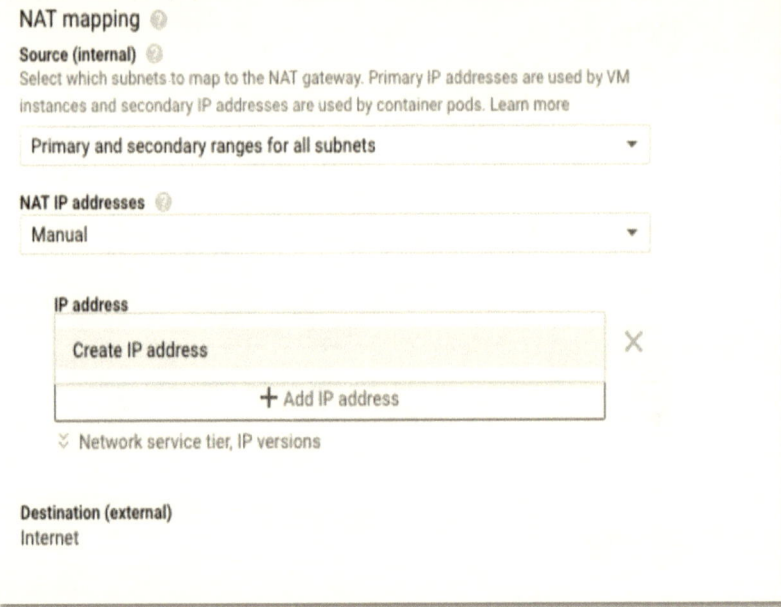

- Select Create IP address and enter the name of the IP address.

Figure 11 – Create Static IP address

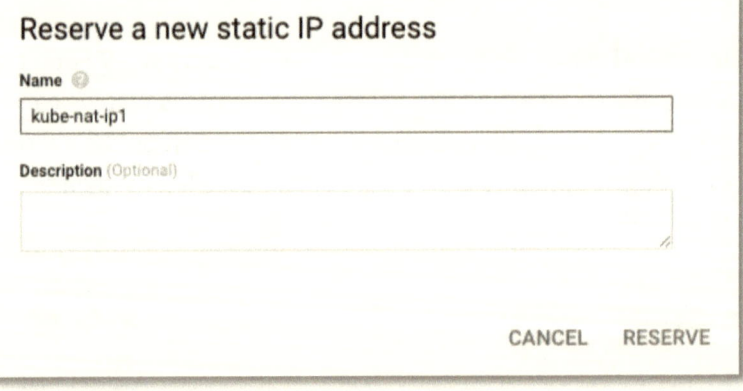

- Similarly, create one more IP address. Two external outbound IPs are sufficient for our network. You can add new IPs based later, if you identify bottlenecks (through monitoring) in your network.

- The following image shows the summary of NAT configuration. Click create.

Figure 12 – NAT Gateway configuration

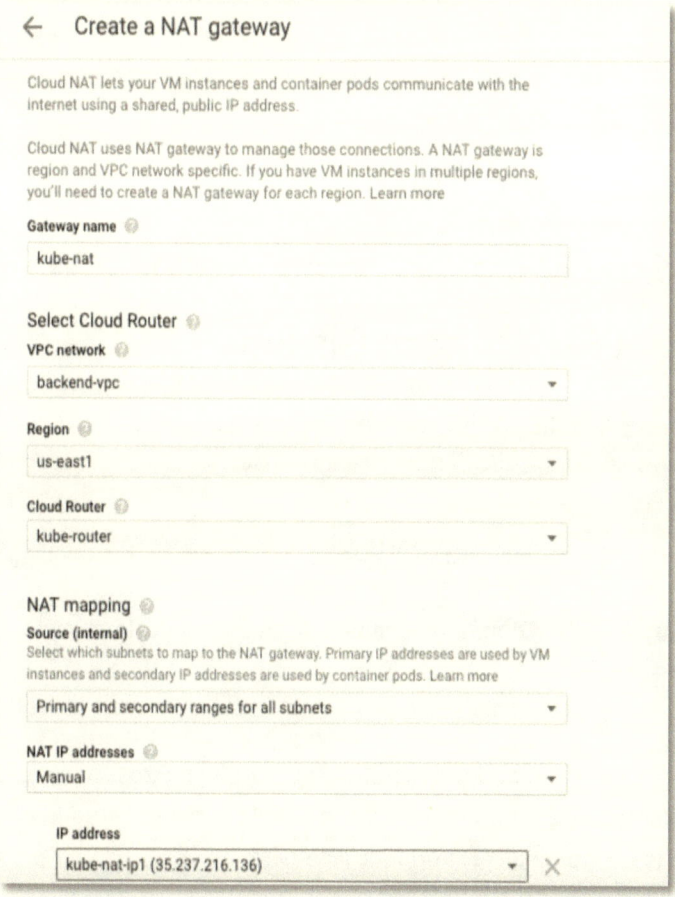

- Once created, wait until the status is Running for changes to be effective.

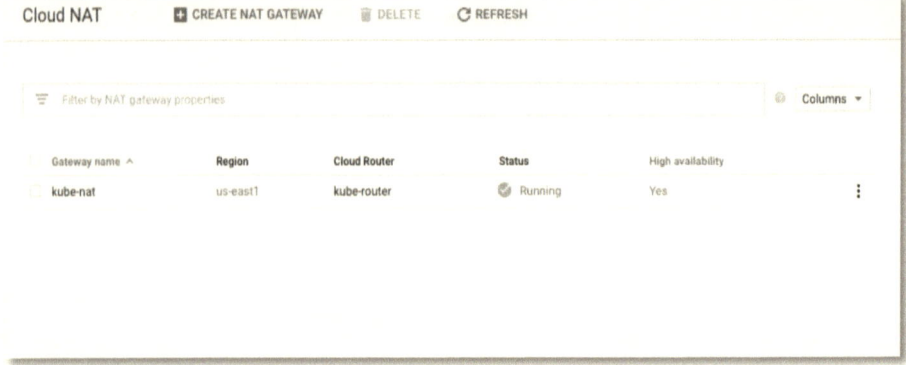

Figure 13 – Cloud NAT Status

Download the Microservice application and Deployment Scripts from GitHub

In this section we would go through the microservices application and deploy the application on the Kubernetes Cluster.

- Download the project from GitHub.

git clone https://github.com/navveenbalani/google-cloud-kubernetes-secure-e2e.git

- Go to the google-cloud-kubernetes-secure-e2e microservice folder. Our microservice comprises of these simple services listed in server.js - echo, healthz, and fecthWebsite.

    Echo service listens over POST and sends the request message back as a response:

```
app.post('/echo', (req, res) => {
  res
    .status(200)
    .json({message: req.body.message})
    .end();
});
```

The healthz service provides a health status for our services. A Service exposed through an Ingress must respond to health checks from the load balancer. We would specify this URL in the readinessProbe configuration while deploying our service.

The fetchWebsite tests out external connectivity from our private Kubernetes cluster. This basically checks if Cloud NAT is configured properly.

```
app.get('/fetchWebsite', (req, res) => {

  request('https://navveenbalani.dev/', function (error, response, html) {
    if (!error && response.statusCode == 200) {
      res
       .status(200)
       .json({message: "ok"})
       .end();
    } else {
          res
       .status(500)
       .json({message: error})
       .end();
    }
  })
});
```

You can deploy your own microservices application but add healthz (or a similar health checkup service) to indicate that the service is healthy and ready.

Build the Microservice Container

In this section, we would build the container. Go to the google-cloud-kubernetes-secure-e2e/microservice folder and execute the following command:

a) Build the docker container
> sudo docker build -t kube-e2e-solution .

b) Run the container
> sudo docker run -p 49180:8080 -d kube-e2e-solution

c) Execute the service
> curl -i http://localhost:49180/healthz
You should see a 200-status message as shown below.

Figure 14 – Output of curl invocation command

```
-e2e$ curl -i http://localhost:49180/healthz
HTTP/1.1 200 OK
X-Powered-By: Express
Content-Type: application/json; charset=utf-8
Content-Length: 16
ETag: W/"10-/VnJyQBB0+b7i4NY83P42KKVWsM"
Date: Mon, 22 Jul 2019 10:13:05 GMT
Connection: keep-alive

{"message":"ok"}navveenbalani@instance-naveen-experiment:~/google-cloud-k
-e2e$ curl -i http://localhost:49180/fetchWebsite
HTTP/1.1 200 OK
X-Powered-By: Express
Content-Type: application/json; charset=utf-8
Content-Length: 16
ETag: W/"10-/VnJyQBB0+b7i4NY83P42KKVWsM"
Date: Mon, 22 Jul 2019 10:13:37 GMT
Connection: keep-alive

{"message":"ok"}navveenbalani@instance-naveen-experiment:~/google-cloud-k
```

Push the Microservice Container to the Google Container Registry

In this section, we would push the container created in earlier step to Google Container Registry. Google Container Registry provides secure private registry and access controls for your docker containers.

Follow the steps below -

i) Tag the image.

> sudo docker tag kube-e2e-solution gcr.io/navveen-api/kube-e2e-solution:v1

This assumes that we would be deploying the container to the gcr.io region. Replace navveen-api by our project name. For deploying to other regions, please refer to https://cloud.google.com/container-registry/docs/pushing-and-pulling.

ii) Create a short lived Access Token to push to container registry (For more details, kindly refer to - https://cloud.google.com/container-registry/docs/advanced-authentication).

> sudo gcloud auth print-access-token | sudo docker login -u oauth2accesstoken --password-stdin https://gcr.io

Figure 15 – Output of access login token command

```
navveenbalani@instance-naveen-experiment:~$ sudo gcloud auth print-access
-token | sudo docker login -u oauth2accesstoken --password-stdin https://
gcr.io
WARNING! Your password will be stored unencrypted in /home/navveenbalani/
.docker/config.json.
Configure a credential helper to remove this warning. See
https://docs.docker.com/engine/reference/commandline/login/#credentials-s
tore

Login Succeeded
navveenbalani@instance-naveen-experiment:~$
```

iii) Push the image to your project (in this case below, navveen-api is the project name).

> sudo docker push gcr.io/navveen-api/kube-e2e-solution:v1

You should see the digest being printed as shown below.

Figure 16 – Output of Docker push command

```
navveenbalani@instance-naveen-experiment:~$ sudo docker push gcr.io/navveen-api/kube-e2
e-solution:v1
The push refers to repository [gcr.io/navveen-api/kube-e2e-solution]
521a3616e73a: Pushed
ebf362c9c68d: Layer already exists
84b71195323c: Layer already exists
9c071f81f2c2: Layer already exists
63983a9db12d: Layer already exists
f03f5e205f59: Layer already exists
4fe39c958fc9: Layer already exists
84d0c4b192e8: Layer already exists
a637c551a0da: Layer already exists
2c8d31157b81: Layer already exists
7b76d801397d: Layer already exists
f32868cde90b: Layer already exists
0db06dff9d9a: Layer already exists
v1: digest: sha256:466bbedd709910aa71a44f6ba4af4a2ff84af933b5998ed041593089c80ffd02 siz
e: 3047
navveenbalani@instance-naveen-experiment:~$
```

Deploy Endpoint for the Application

Next, we would deploy the endpoint configuration for our microservices application. As mentioned earlier, we are using Cloud Endpoints for API management to secure, monitor, analyze, and set quotas on our APIs. Endpoints support version 2 of the OpenAPI Specification. For more details, refer to https://cloud.google.com/endpoints/docs/openapi/.

The OpenAPI configuration file of our microservice project is provided in script/kube-openapi-backend.yaml.

Open kube-openapi-backend.yaml and replace the host "apis.navveenbalani.dev" with the hostname where your API would be available. My APIs are available at apis.navveenbalani.dev. If you don't have a host readily available, you can use <api-name>.endpoints.<YOUR-PROJECT-ID>.cloud.goog in host name, replace api-name with the name for your api and YOUR-PROJECT-ID with your google project id. You can later use the host name and map it to the IP address in your DNS settings and use the host name to invoke your service. For more details, refer to Configuring DNS for Endpoints section at https://cloud.google.com/endpoints/docs/openapi/get-started-kubernetes#configuring-endpoints-dns.

Next, we would deploy the endpoints for the application by following the steps below:
- Install Google Cloud SDK (if you haven't already) from https://cloud.google.com/sdk/) on your local machine.
- With Google SDK installed, open a command prompt and set the project. Replace navveen-api with your project id.

    > gcloud config set project navveen-api

- Go to scripts folder. Deploy the endpoint configuration by running the following command: -

    > gcloud endpoints services deploy kube-openapi-backend.yaml

You should see similar messages being printed on the console and a URL being provided at the end to manage your APIs.

Figure 17 – Output of endpoint deployment

```
navveenbalani@instance-navveen-experiment:~/google-cloud-kubernetes-secure-e2e/scripts$
sudo gcloud endpoints services deploy kube-openapi-backend.yaml
Waiting for async operation operations/serviceConfigs.apis.navveenbalani.dev:7feffb69-d
075-4e84-981f-af1bd13c7f23 to complete...
Operation finished successfully. The following command can describe the Operation detai
ls:
 gcloud endpoints operations describe operations/serviceConfigs.apis.navveenbalani.dev:
7feffb69-d075-4e84-981f-af1bd13c7f23

WARNING: kube-openapi-backend.yaml: Operation 'get' in path '/auth/info/googleidtoken':
 Operation does not require an API key; callers may invoke the method without specifyin
g an associated API-consuming project. To enable API key all the SecurityRequirement Ob
jects (https://github.com/OAI/OpenAPI-Specification/blob/master/versions/2.0.md#securit
y-requirement-object) inside security definition must reference at least one SecurityDe
finition of type : 'apiKey'.

WARNING: kube-openapi-backend.yaml: Operation 'get' in path '/auth/info/googlejwt': Ope
ration does not require an API key; callers may invoke the method without specifying an
 associated API-consuming project. To enable API key all the SecurityRequirement Object
s (https://github.com/OAI/OpenAPI-Specification/blob/master/versions/2.0.md#security-re
quirement-object) inside security definition must reference at least one SecurityDefini
tion of type : 'apiKey'.

Waiting for async operation operations/rollouts.apis.navveenbalani.dev:ada3f5e9-a7de-41
5d-bc09-f06e0bdeb1e1 to complete...
Operation finished successfully. The following command can describe the Operation detai
ls:
 gcloud endpoints operations describe operations/rollouts.apis.navveenbalani.dev:ada3f5
e9-a7de-415d-bc09-f06e0bdeb1e1

Service Configuration [2019-07-22r0] uploaded for service [apis.navveenbalani.dev]

To manage your API, go to: https://console.cloud.google.com/endpoints/api/apis.navveenb
alani.dev/overview?project=navveen-api
```

- Next, create an API key to access the Endpoint. Go to https://console.cloud.google.com/apis/credentials and select your GCP project.
- Click Create credentials, and then select API key,
- Copy the key to the clipboard. We will use the API key later when calling our endpoint.
- You can further apply restrictions on the API key (like HTTP Referrer, IP address, devices etc.) on who can invoke your endpoint based on your application needs. For instance, if you want to ensure your application can be invoked by specific IP

addresses only, you can specify the list of IP addresses by clicking on the IP address option.

Create Workload, Service and Ingress

In this section, we would create the workload, service, and Ingress for our application. Go to the scripts folder of google-cloud-kubernetes-secure-e2e/scripts project and run the following commands in google cloud sdk/shell.

1. Set the project. Replace Navveen-api by your project id.

   > gcloud config set project navveen-api

2. Connect to backend-custer

   > gcloud container clusters get-credentials backend-cluster --zone us-east1-b

   The backend-cluster is the kubernetes cluster and zone is us-east1-b where our cluster is running.

3. Deploying the workload (backend)
o The kube-backend-deployment-gcp.yaml deploys our microservices container (kube-e2e-service) and kube-esp (google endpoint runtime container) as shown below.

   ```
   containers:
   - name: kube-e2e-service
     image: gcr.io/navveen-api/kube-e2e-solution:v1
     ports:
     - containerPort: 8080
   ```

```yaml
- name: kube-esp
  image: gcr.io/endpoints-release/endpoints-runtime:1
  args: [
    "--http_port", "8081",
    "--backend", "127.0.0.1:8080",
    "--service", "apis.navveenbalani.dev",
    "--rollout_strategy", "managed",
  ]
  readinessProbe:
    httpGet:
      path: /healthz?key=AIzaSyC0m7d4cc-jOwJIzymv9ntObF1ukIMrTc-
      port: 8081
    initialDelaySeconds: 60
  livenessProbe:
    httpGet:
      path: /healthz?key=AIzaSyC0m7d4cc-jOwJIzymv9ntObF1ukIMrTc-
      port: 8081
    initialDelaySeconds: 60
  ports:
    - containerPort: 8081
```

All incoming requests would first be intercepted by the google endpoint container (kube-esp) which would will direct them to the microservices container (kube-e2e-service). The google endpoint container checks the API key and any rule that you have applied on the API key (quotas, IP address restriction, device restrictions etc.) and then forwards the request to respective endpoints in the microservices container.

o   Open the kube-backend-deployment-gcp.yaml and replace "apis.navveenbalani.dev" with the hostname you provided in Step 7 while configuring the endpoint. The service name determines which endpoint configuration should be called.

- o   Replace AIzaSyC0m7d4cc-jOwJIzymv9ntObF1ukIMrTc- with the endpoint API key that you generated in earlier step.

- o   The readinessProbe and livenessProbe defines the health check URL for our service. Once the container is started, the path mentioned in the URL would be invoked, and if the response is 200, the container would be in ready state and should start serving requests. Note, this would test the endpoint configuration, as well as the actual microservice endpoint. We had discussed health check URLs in Step 4 earlier, and through this configuration, we decide which service to invoke for a health check.

- o   Deploy the workload by running the following command.

    > kubectl apply -f kube-backend-deployment-gcp.yaml

- o   Navigate to Kubernetes Engine -> Workload and you should see the status as green in a few minutes as shown below once the heath check is done.

Figure 18 – Status of workloads

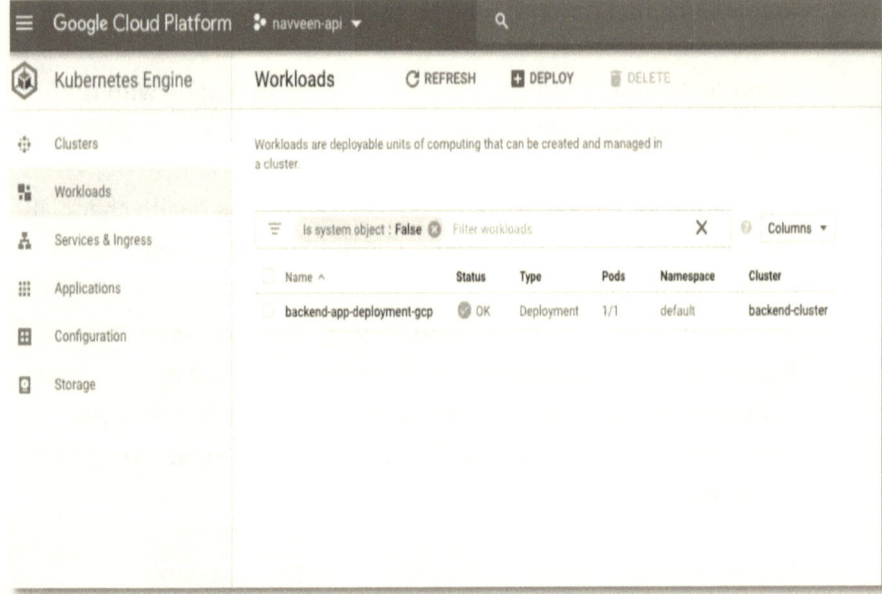

4. Deploying the service
    o The kube-backend-service-node-gcp.yaml exposes the service on each Node IP at a static port (using NodePort type). The port:8081 is the static port and targetPort:8081 is the port where the request needs to be sent, which is the kube-esp container that we discussed earlier.

    ```
    spec:
     type: NodePort
     selector:
       apps: backend-gcp
     ports:
     - port: 8081
       targetPort: 8081
    ```

    o Create the service by running the following command.

> kubectl apply -f kube-backend-service-node-gcp.yaml

5. Creating Ingress

In Kubernetes, an Ingress is a resource that allows access to your services from outside the Kubernetes cluster. Ingress resource consists of two components - a set of rules and an Ingress Controller.
The set of rules allows inbound connections to be directed to specific services in Kubernetes. An Ingress controller, which is typically configured as an HTTP Load Balancer implements the rules and direct connections to the respective services.

Follow the steps below to create Ingress for our application.

- First, we would create a static IP for Http Load balancer. Go to VPC Network - External IP addresses -> Reserve Static Address. Enter a name for IP (copy it, as we will use this later) and select type as Global. LoadBalancer works only with Global Type.

Figure 20 – Create Static IP address

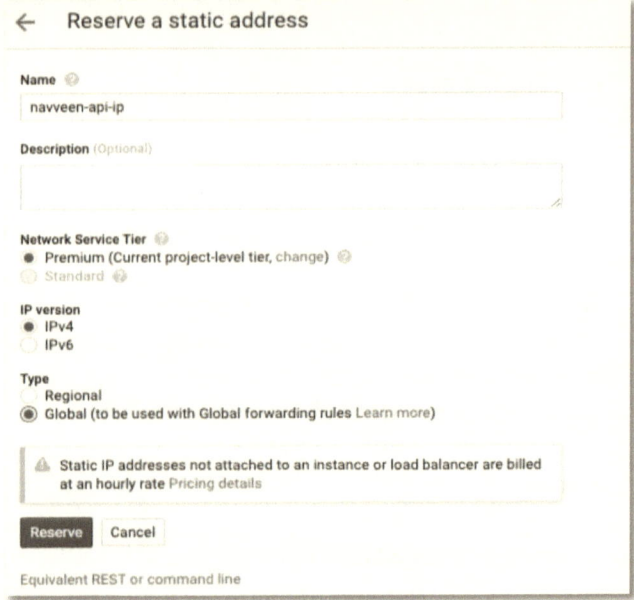

- Click Reserve and note the IP address. This is our external IP address where the service would be exposed. I have mapped this IP to my host api.navveenbalani.dev (in DNS). You can map this IP to your host name where apis would be available.

- Our services would be exposed over HTTPS (i.e. for my configuration it's as https://api.naveenbalani.dev).

    Next, we would create the SSL secret configuration, which consists of certificate and key for your domain. This assumes that you already have the SSL certificates, otherwise you can generate one using third party SSL provides like letsencrypt. Run the following command

```
kubectl create secret tls kube-api-ssl-secret \
  --cert /Users/naveenbalani/Downloads/api-naveenbalani-dev-ssl/certificate-merged.crt --key /Users/naveenbalani/Downloads/api-naveenbalani-dev-ssl/private.key
```

Where /Users/naveenbalani/Downloads/api-naveenbalani-dev-ssl/certificate-merged.crt is path to the certificate and /Users/naveenbalani/Downloads/api-naveenbalani-dev-ssl/private.key is the path to the private key

- Next, we will deploy the Ingress. Ingress configuration is provided in the kube-backend-ingress-ssl-gcp.yaml file. Open the file and replace "navveen-api-ip" with the static IP address name that we created in earlier step. Also replace apis.navveenbalani.dev with your host name. We also reference the SSL secret "kube-api-ssl-secret" that we created earlier for the host apis.navveenbalani.dev. We also define a rule, that all request to apis.navveenbalani.dev would be directed to kube-node-service-gcp (i.e. NodePort) that we created in Deploying the service section earlier.

```yaml
kind: Ingress
metadata:
  name: kube-ingress-gcp
  annotations:
    kubernetes.io/ingress.allow-http: "true"
    kubernetes.io/ingress.global-static-ip-name: navveen-api-ip
spec:
  tls:
  - hosts:
    - apis.navveenbalani.dev
    secretName: kube-api-ssl-secret
  rules:
```

```
         - host: apis.navveenbalani.dev
           http:
             paths:
             - backend:
                   serviceName: kube-node-service-gcp
                   servicePort: 8081
```

- Run the following command to create Ingress.

   ```
   > kubectl apply -f kube-backend-ingress-ssl-gcp.yaml
   ```

- Go to Kubernetes Engine - > Services and Ingress in Google cloud console and inspect the Ingress configuration. You should see the status of "kube-ingress-gcp" green in some time.

Figure 22 – Status of Services & Ingress

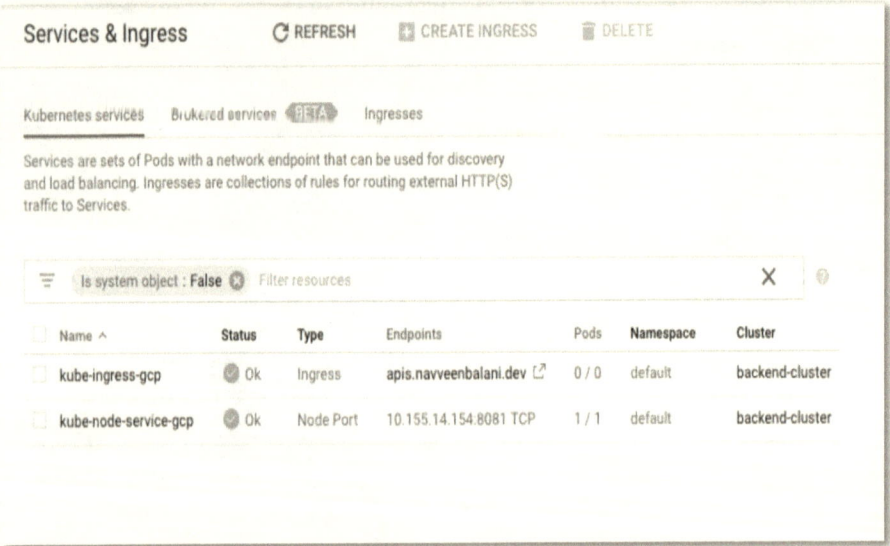

- Click on kube-ingress gcp. Click on the backend services and select the backend service where service port is 8081.

Figure 23 – Ingress Detail

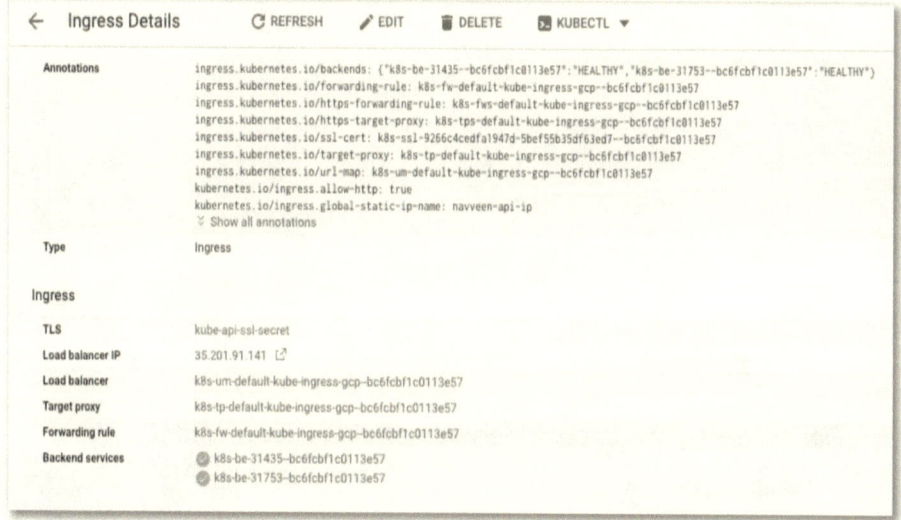

Figure 24 – Ingress Detail -> Backend: Port 8081

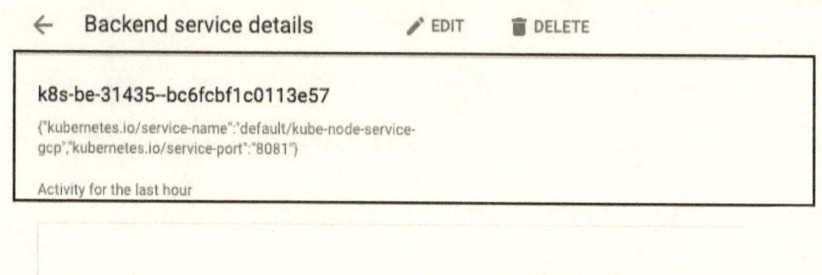

- Next, click on the Health check link and on the Heath check page you, should see the path (i.e look for Path variable) that we have specified in the workload deployment file being used for the health check.

Figure 25 – Ingress Backend Service - > Heath Check

Protocol
HTTP

In use by
k8s-um-default-kube-ingress-gcp--bc6fcbf1c0113e57

Timeout
How long to wait for the backend service to respond before considering it a failed request

30 seconds

Backends
1 instance group

Health check
k8s-be-31435--bc6fcbf1c0113e57
port: 31435, timeout: 1s, check interval: 70s, unhealthy threshold: 10 attempts

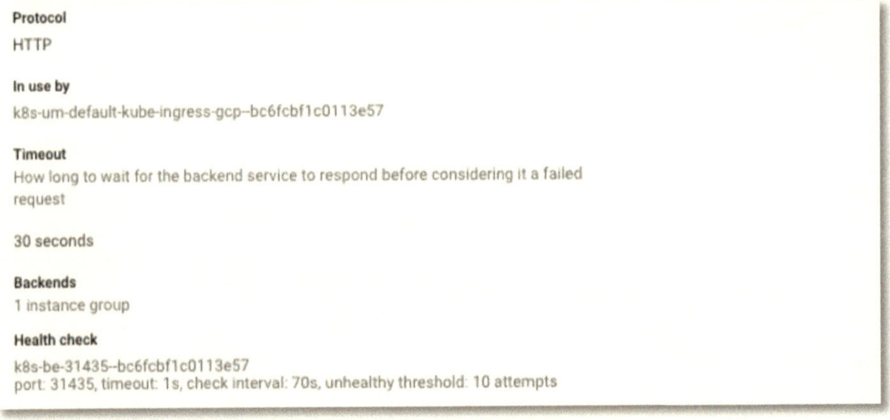

Figure 26 – Ingress Backend Service - > Heath Check -> Path

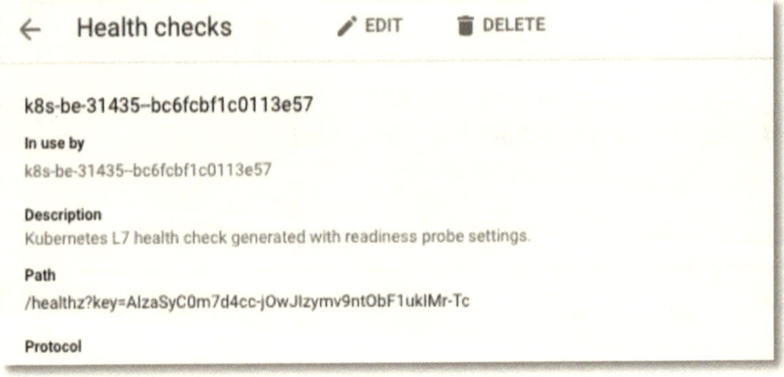

← Health checks   ✏ EDIT   🗑 DELETE

k8s-be-31435--bc6fcbf1c0113e57

In use by
k8s-be-31435--bc6fcbf1c0113e57

Description
Kubernetes L7 health check generated with readiness probe settings.

Path
/healthz?key=AIzaSyC0m7d4cc-jOwJIzymv9ntObF1ukIMr-Tc

Protocol

With this, we have setup the Ingress. Next, we would invoke our microservice.

Invoke the Microservices

In this step, we would invoke the microservices. You can use a tool like CURL to invoke the echo microservice as shown below.

```
> curl --request POST \
  --header "content-type:application/json" \
  --data '{"message":"hello echo"}' \
       "https://apis.navveenbalani.dev/echo?key=AlzaSyC0m7d4cc-jOwJ"
```

(replace AlzaSyC0m7d4cc-jOwJ with your endpoint key)

You would see the response message being printed in the console.

Next, execute the fetchWebsite service.

```
> curl -i
https://apis.navveenbalani.dev/fetchWebsite?key=AlzaSyC0m7d4cc-jOwJ
```

You would see the message "ok' being printed on the console, denoting that your service can access internet (external IP) from your private kubernetes cluster through Cloud NAT.

Figure 27: Output of curl invocation

```
HTTP/1.1 200 OK
Server: nginx
Date: Tue, 02 Jul 2019 11:47:46 GMT
Content-Type: application/json; charset=utf-8
Content-Length: 16
X-Powered-By: Express
ETag: W/"10-/VnJyQBB0+b7i4NY83P42KKVWsM"
Via: 1.1 google
Alt-Svc: clear

{"message":"ok"}Naveens-MacBook-Air:google-cloud-kubernetes-secure-e2e
```

Next, we would whitelist the IPs that can access our service. We would use Cloud Armor and configure it with our kubernetes cluster.

Configure Cloud Armor

Google Cloud Armor works with Global HTTP(S) Load Balancer to provide built-in defenses against infrastructure DDoS attacks. It provides IP and geo-based access control and a set of rich rules (currently in alpha) to defend against cross-site scripting (XSS) and SQL injection defense.

Let's create Cloud Armor configuration for our application. To demonstrate, we would use IP whitelisting to all IPs for now and invoke our application. We would later change the configuration to deny all IP address that should provide an unauthorized error.

Go to Network Security > Click Cloud Armor -> Click Create Policy

Figure 28: Cloud Armor -> Create Policy

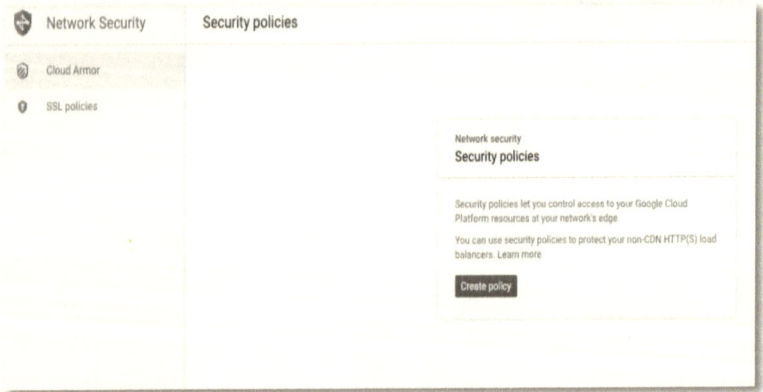

- Enter the name in the policy and select Allow in rule action.

    Figure 29: Cloud Armor -> Policy Details

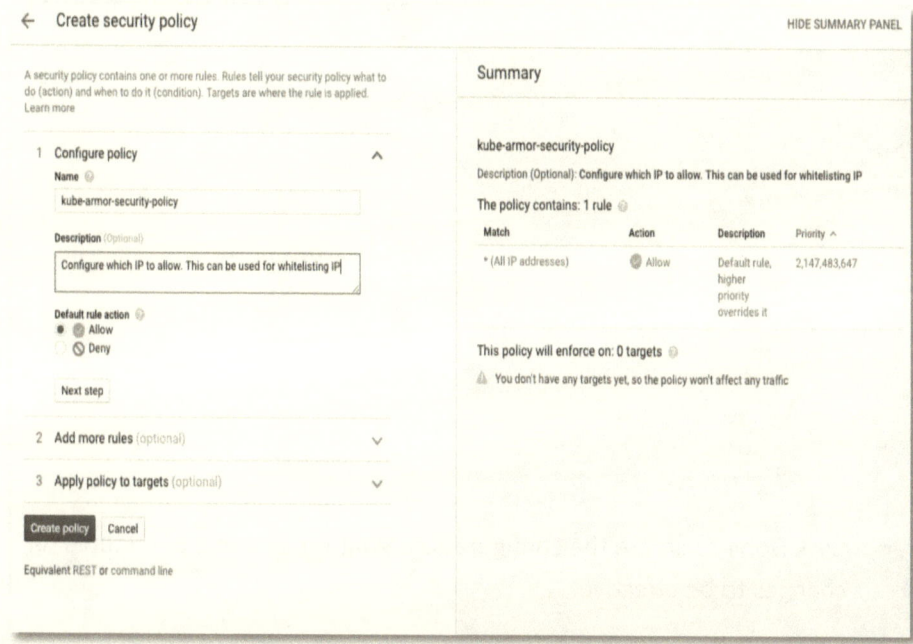

- Click Next Step and enter ip - 0.0.0.0/0 (to allow all ip address) in the match and priority as 0 (executed first) as shown in figure below.

Figure 30: Cloud Armor -> Policy Details -> IP Details

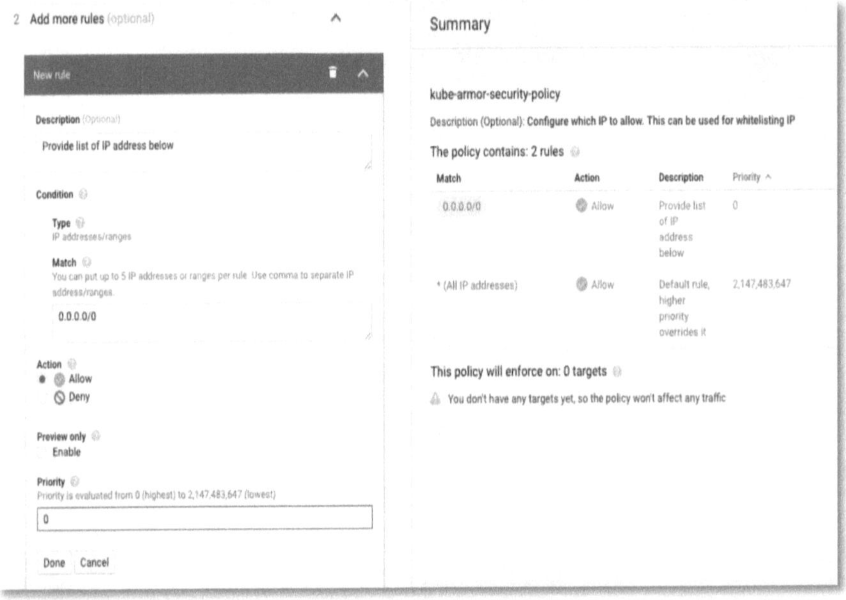

- Click Done to create the configuration. Wait for a couple of minutes for changes to be effective.

- Next, we would add the configuration created above to our kubernetes cluster. We need to create a BackendConfig as shown below which references the "kube-armor-security-policy" created earlier and later add the BackendConfig configuration to our service configuration.

```
apiVersion: cloud.google.com/v1beta1
kind: BackendConfig
metadata:
  namespace: default
  name: kube-armor-config
spec:
  securityPolicy:
    name: "kube-armor-security-policy"
```

Run the command to create the backend configuration.

> kubectl apply -f kube-backend-armor-gcp.yaml

- Then, delete the existing kube-node-service-gcp by navigating to Kubernetes Engine > Services & Ingress in cloud console. We would create a new configuration with the cloud armor backend configuration created in the earlier step.

Figure 31: Service & Ingress -> Select & Delete

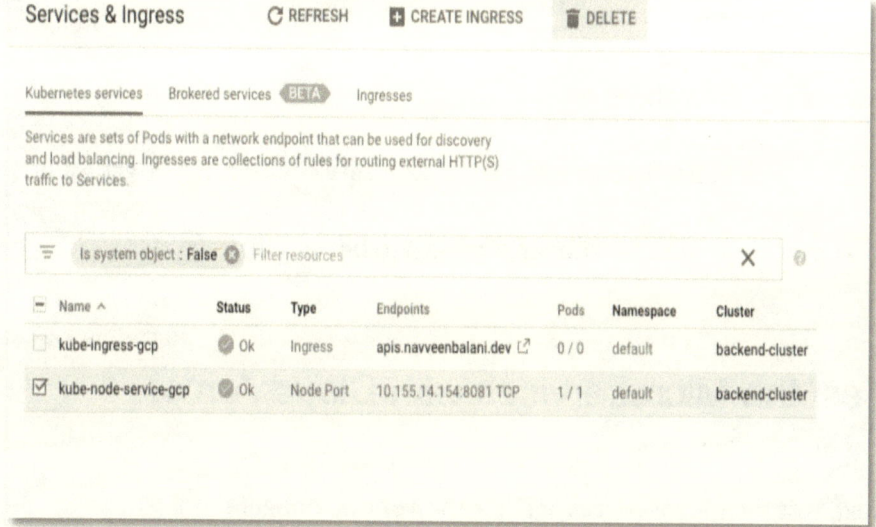

- Afterward, run the kube-backend-service-node-armor-gcp.yaml file. The contents of the file are the same as the kube-backend-service-node-gcp.yaml file with the additional backend-config annotation that references the kube-armor-config created in the earlier step.

```
metadata:
  name: kube-node-service-gcp
```

```
  labels:
    apps: backend-gcp
  annotations:
    beta.cloud.google.com/backend-config: '{"ports": {"8081":"kube-armor-config"}}'
spec:
  type: NodePort
  selector:
    apps: backend-gcp
  ports:
  - port: 8081
    targetPort: 8081
```

Execute the command –

> kubectl apply -f kube-backend-service-node-armor-gcp.yaml

After execution, wait for kube-ingress-gcp to be back in green state.

Test the Microservices with Cloud Armor

Next, test the microservices again with the new configuration.

> curl -i https://apis.navveenbalani.dev/fetchWebsite?key=AlzaSyC0m7d4cc-jOwJ

You should see the message "ok' being printed on the console.

Next, go to Cloud Console -> Network Security -> Cloud Armor and click on the kube-armor-security-policy. On the kube-armor-security-policy page, click Logs to view the request logs. You can inspect each incoming request (headers, message, ip address etc.) in detail by inspecting the logs.

Figure 32: Cloud Armor Logs

```
▼ 🛈 2019-07-02 17:45:46.392 IST  GET  200    252 B    null curl/7.58.. https://apis.navveenbalani.dev/fetchWebsite?
                                       key=AIzaSyC0m7d4cc-j0wJIzymv9ntObFlukIMr-Tc
    103.58.10.68 - "GET https://apis.navveenbalani.dev/fetchWebsite?key=AIzaSyC0m7d4cc-j0wJIzymv9ntObFlukIMr-Tc" 200 252 "curl/7.58.0"

  ▼ {                                                                                Expand all | Collapse all
    ▼ httpRequest: {
        remoteIp: "103.58.10.68"
        requestMethod: "GET"
        requestSize: "142"
        requestUrl: "https://apis.navveenbalani.dev/fetchWebsite?key=AIzaSyC0m7d4cc-j0wJIzymv9ntObFlukIMr-Tc"
        responseSize: "252"
        serverIp: "10.0.0.4"
        status: 200
        userAgent: "curl/7.58.0"
      }
      insertId: "1uvhd9kg169vryr"
    ▶ jsonPayload: {…}
      logName: "projects/navveen-api/logs/requests"
      receiveTimestamp: "2019-07-02T12:15:47.1872965602"
    ▶ resource: {…}
      severity: "INFO"
      spanId: "10ce10251377b033"
      timestamp: "2019-07-02T12:15:46.392240089Z"
```

To test out IP whitelisting, modify the existing Kube-armor-security-policy Policy. Click on Edit rule and select deny instead of allow as shown below. Then, click update.

Figure 33: Cloud Armor -> Policy Details - > Deny All

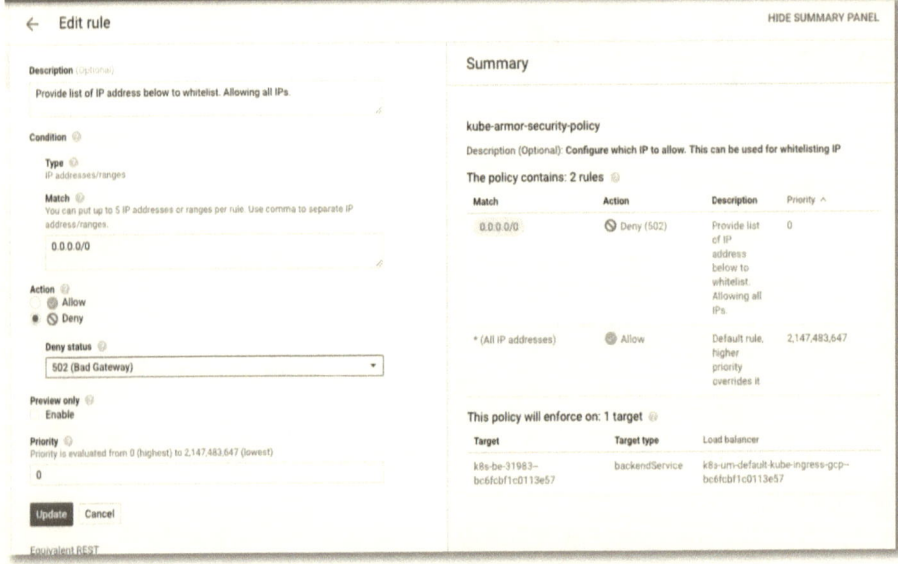

Wait for a few minutes for changes to be effective.

Next, execute the fetchWebsite service.

> curl -i https://apis.navveenbalani.dev/fetchWebsite?key=AlzaSyC0m7d4cc-jOwJ

You should see 502 Bad Gateway as a response as shown below.

Figure 34: Bad Gateway error

```
HTTP/1.1 502 Bad Gateway
Content-Length: 136
Content-Type: text/html; charset=UTF-8
Date: Tue, 02 Jul 2019 12:24:25 GMT
Alt-Svc: clear
```

With this, we have tested IP whitelisting. Change the configuration back to allow all IP Addresses.

Building the Solution 2 - Using Nginx Ingress Controller

In this chapter, we would deploy Nginx Ingress Controller instead of GCE.

NGINX, by default, provides a lot of additional capabilities as compared to the default GKE Ingress controller like URL rewriting, whitelisting, load balancing over HTTPS and websocket and advanced features through Nginx Plus. For details, refer to https://www.nginx.com/products/nginx/.

It is assumed that you have executed Step 1 - 7 of Solution 1.

Install Nginx Ingress

The first step is to install Nginx Ingress in our cluster. Navigate to Cloud Console -> Kubernetes Engine -> Cluster. Click on the connect button for backend-cluster. This will launch the cloud shell as shown below. Click ok to Run in cloud shell to connect to the backend-cluster.

Figure 35: Cloud Shell

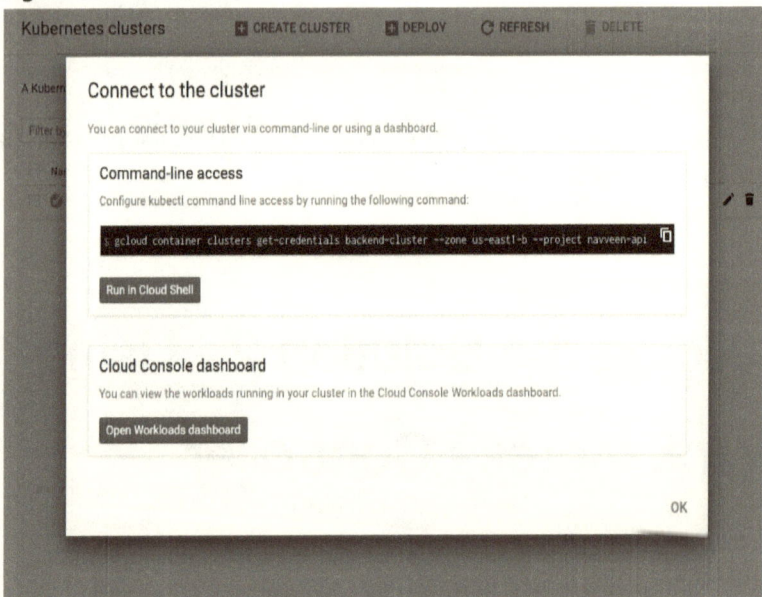

Next, we will install Helm which allows us to install and manage Kubernetes applications and resources effectively. Helm has two parts: a client (helm) which runs on cloud shell and a server (tiller) which runs inside of the kubernetes cluster and manages the installation.

Install the latest version of Helm by running the following command:

```
> curl -o get_helm.sh https://raw.githubusercontent.com/kubernetes/helm/master/scripts/get
> chmod +x get_helm.sh
> ./get_helm.sh
```

Next, we would Install Tiller. Run the following commands to install the server-side tiller to the Kubernetes cluster. The below command creates a service account and the cluster-admin role to manage the cluster.

> kubectl create serviceaccount --namespace kube-system tiller

> kubectl create clusterrolebinding tiller-cluster-rule --clusterrole=cluster-admin --serviceaccount=kube-system:tiller

> helm init --service-account tiller

The following image shows the command interactions and output at the google cloud shell.

Figure 36: Cloud Shell -> Installation of Helm

```
            @cloudshell:~ (navveen-api)$ chmod +x get_helm.sh
            @cloudshell:~ (navveen-api)$ ./get_helm.sh
Helm v2.14.1 is already latest
Run 'helm init' to configure helm.
            @cloudshell:~ (navveen-api)$ kubectl create serviceaccount --
serviceaccount/tiller created
            @cloudshell:~ (navveen-api)$ kubectl create clusterrolebindi
clusterrolebinding.rbac.authorization.k8s.io/tiller-cluster-rule created
            @cloudshell:~ (navveen-api)$ helm init --service-account til
Creating /home/          /.helm
Creating /home/          /.helm/repository
Creating /home/          /.helm/repository/cache
Creating /home/          /.helm/repository/local
Creating /home/          /.helm/plugins
Creating /home/          /.helm/starters
Creating /home/          /.helm/cache/archive
Creating /home/          /.helm/repository/repositories.yaml
Adding stable repo with URL: https://kubernetes-charts.storage.googleap:
Adding local repo with URL: http://127.0.0.1:8879/charts
$HELM_HOME has been configured at /home/          /.helm.

Tiller (the Helm server-side component) has been installed into your Kul

Please note: by default, Tiller is deployed with an insecure 'allow una
To prevent this, run `helm init` with the --tiller-tls-verify flag.
```

Next, we will install the Nginx Ingress through Helm. Installing Nginx Ingress will configure a Service type of LoadBalancer in our cluster which will route all the incoming requests as per the rules you define in the deployment file (we will look at this later while deploying the ingress.yaml file).

LoadBalancer should listen over an IP. The IP can be automatically assigned by the network system or you can create a static IP address and use the ip address while installing Nginx. We will create a static IP address since this IP address can then be mapped to your domain name where you want to expose the service for public consumption (i.e. similar to domain like api.naveenbalani.dev that we went through in Solution 1). SSL certificate can also be installed on the domain, so you can receive HTTPS requests.

Create a static IP address of type Regional and select the region (select the same region as that of your VPN). Please note that Global Type would not work with Nginx Ingress LoadBalancer. Following image shows the configuration.

Figure 37: Create Static IP

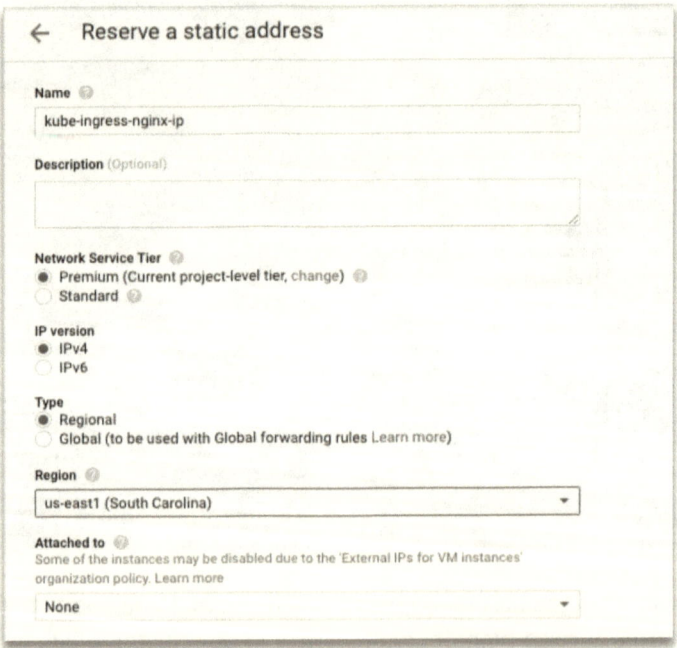

Create the IP and note the IP address.

Next, go back to cloud shell and install Nginx Ingress by running the following command. Replace 35.231.11.11 by the IP from the earlier step.

```
> helm install --name nginx-ingress stable/nginx-ingress \
    --set controller.service.loadBalancerIP=35.231.11.11\
    --set rbac.create=true \
    --set controller.publishService.enabled=true
```

The above command would create a Nginx Ingress Controller of type HTTP Load Balancer at 35.231.11.11.

You can also enable SSL while installing Nginx Ingress. If you have an SSL certificate for your domain, you can enable SSL while installing Nginx ingress.

First, you need to create the secret based on your domain certificate and private key.

```
> kubectl create secret tls backend-api-ssl-secret \
  --cert /Users/navveenbalani/<domain.com>/certificate.crt --key /Users/navveenbalani/<domain.com>/private.key
```

Next, you need to reference the backend-api-ssl-secret while installing Nginx Ingress. Use the following command to enable SSL during installation:

```
helm install --name nginx-ingress stable/nginx-ingress \
    --set controller.service.loadBalancerIP=35.231.11.11\
    --set rbac.create=true \
    --set controller.publishService.enabled=true \
    --set controller.extraArgs.default-ssl-
      certificate=default/backend-ssl-secret
```

After running the command, you should get the following message on the console:

The nginx-ingress controller has been installed.
It may take a few minutes for the LoadBalancer IP to be available.

To see the status of the Nginx Ingress controller, run the following command:

> kubectl --namespace default get services -o wide -w nginx-ingress-controller

If you see an external IP (the one that we provided earlier), that implies the Nginx Controller is listening on the configured external IP.

Figure 38: Nginx Ingress Status

```
(navveen-api)$ kubectl get service nginx-ingress-controller
  TYPE              CLUSTER-IP      EXTERNAL-IP     PORT(S)
  LoadBalancer     10.155.1.133    35.231.11.11    80:30055/TCP,443:30771/TCP
(navveen-api)$
```

If you navigate to Kubernetes Engine -> Service & Ingress, you will see nginx-ingress-controller listening on the ip address that we configured earlier as shown in the figure below. You would also see a service named "nginx-ingress-default-backend". The nginx-ingress-default-backend service provides default backend which handles all URL paths and hosts the nginx controller doesn't understand (i.e., all the requests that are not mapped with an Ingress). Basically, a default backend exposes two URLs: - /healthz that returns 200 and / that return 404. You can use the Nginx default backend service for the health check instead of providing your own heath check service implementation, that we discussed earlier in Solution 1.

Figure 39: Nginx Ingress Status in Cloud Console

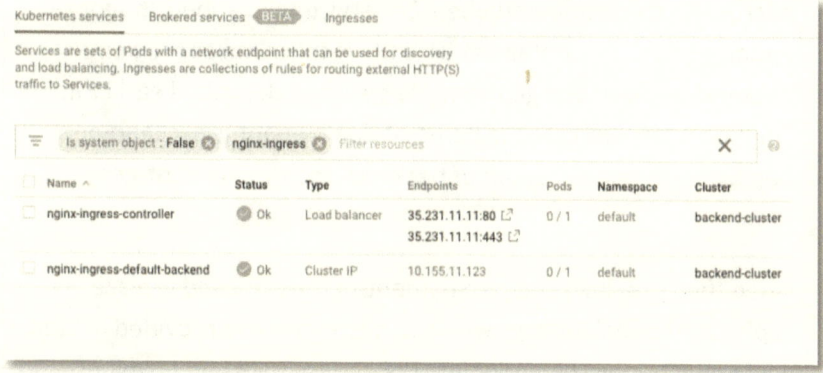

With the Ingress controller setup, we would execute the deployment scripts.

Create Workload, Service and Ingress

Go to the scripts folder of google-cloud-kubernetes-secure-e2e/scripts project and run the following commands in google cloud sdk/shell.

1. Set the project. Replace navveen-api by your project id.
   > gcloud config set project navveen-api

2. Connect to the backend-custer
   > gcloud container clusters get-credentials backend-cluster --zone us-east1-b

   The backend-cluster is the kubernetes cluster and the zone is us-east1-b where our cluster is running.

3. Deploying the workload

- The kube-backend-deployment-nginx.yaml deploys our microservices container (kube-e2e-service) and kube-esp (google endpoint runtime container). This file is the same as the kube-backend-deployment-gcp.yaml that we had described earlier in Solution 1, except that the name of deployment is backend-app-deployment-nginx (instead of backend-app-deployment-gcp).

- Open the kube-backend-deployment-nginx.yaml and replace "apis.navveenbalani.dev" with the hostname you provided in Step 7 while configuring the endpoint. The service name determines which endpoint configuration should be called.

- Replace AlzaSyC0m7d4cc-jOwJIzymv9ntObF1ukIMrTc- with the endpoint API key that you generated in the earlier step.

- The readinessProbe and livenessProbe defines the health check URL for our service. Once the container is started, the path mentioned in the URL would be invoked, and if the response is 200, the container would be in the ready state and start serving requests. Note, this would test the endpoint configuration as well as the actual microservice endpoint. We had discussed the health check URL in Step 4 earlier, and through this configuration, we provide which service to invoke for a health check. If you omit the health check configuration for nginx ingress, it would still work as the default backend service (i.e. nginx-ingress-default-backend service) that we discussed earlier provides a health check service which returns 200.

- Deploy the workload by running the following command.

    > kubectl apply -f kube-backend-deployment-nginx.yaml

- Navigate to Kubernetes Engine -> Workload and you should see the status as green for *backend-app-deployment-nginx* in few minutes.

4. Deploying the service
    o The kube-backend-service-node-nginx.yaml exposes the service on each Node IP at a static port (using NodePort type). The port:8081 is the static port and targetPort:8081 is the port where requests need to be sent, which is the kube-esp container that we discussed earlier.

    ```
    spec:
     type: NodePort
     selector:
       apps: backend-nginx
     ports:
     - port: 8081
       targetPort: 8081
    ```

    o Create the service by running the following command.

    ```
    > kubectl apply -f kube-backend-service-node-nginx.yaml
    ```

5. Creating Ingress

Follow the steps below to create Ingress for our application.

o The Ingress configuration is provided in kube-backend-ingress-nginx.yaml file. This file is similar to kube-backend ingress-ssl-gcp.yaml that we had discussed in Solution 1 earlier. We have added an annotation "kubernetes.io/ingress.class: nginx" to denote we want to use Nginx Ingress instead of GCE.

```
apiVersion: extensions/v1beta1
kind: Ingress
metadata:
```

```
    name: kube-ingress-nginx
    annotations:
      kubernetes.io/ingress.class: nginx
      nginx.ingress.kubernetes.io/ssl-redirect: "false"
  spec:
    rules:
    - http:
        paths:
        - backend:
            serviceName: kube-node-service-nginx
            servicePort: 8081
```

The rules specify that any incoming http request would be directed to kube-node-service-nginx service. The kube-node-service-nginx service would direct it to the endpoint runtime, which would further forward it to the actual microservice implementation.

o   Run the following command to create Ingress.

```
> kubectl apply -f kube-backend-ingress-nginx.yaml
```

o   Go to Kubernetes Engine - > Services and Ingress in Google cloud console and inspect the Ingress configuration. You should see the status of "kube-ngress-nginx" as green in some time.

Figure 40: Service & Ingress Status in Cloud Console

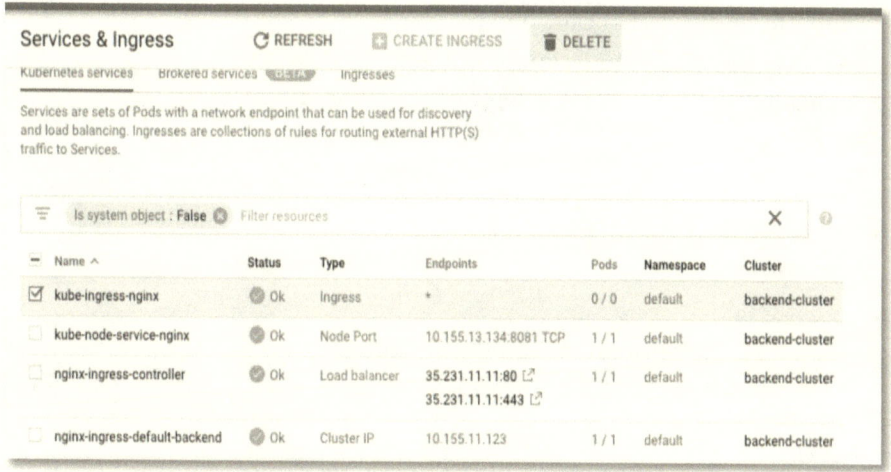

- Test the microservice by invoking the URL and you should see a response "ok" being printed on the console.

  > curl -i http://35.231.11.11:80/fetchWebsite?key=AIzaSyC0m7d4cc-jOwJlzymv9ntObF1ukIMr-Tc

- Next, we would modify our ingress file to whitelist IPs. We add the below annotation with source range as 0.0.0.0/0 to allow IPs.

  nginx.ingress.kubernetes.io/whitelist-source-range: "0.0.0.0/0"

We have created a new file "kube-backend-ingress-whitelist-all-nginx.yaml" which contains the added annotation.

```
apiVersion: extensions/v1beta1
kind: Ingress
metadata:
 name: kube-ingress-nginx
 annotations:
```

53

```
    kubernetes.io/ingress.class: nginx
    nginx.ingress.kubernetes.io/ssl-redirect: "false"
    nginx.ingress.kubernetes.io/whitelist-source-range: "0.0.0.0/0"
spec:
  rules:
  - http:
      paths:
      - backend:
          serviceName: kube-node-service-nginx
          servicePort: 8081
```

- o Before running the new configuration, delete the existing kube-ngress-nginx ingress (by selecting kube-ngress-nginx and clicking delete from the Services & Ingress page). Run the following command to create Ingress.

    > kubectl apply -f kube-backend-ingress-whitelist-all-nginx.yaml

- o Test the microservice again by invoking the URL and you should see a response "ok" being printed on the console. This tests out the whitelisting for our ingress.

    > curl -i http://35.231.11.11:80/fetchWebsite?key=AlzaSyC0m7d4cc-jOwJlzymv9ntObF1uklMr-Tc

- o Next, we would modify our ingress file to whitelist a specific IP. We add the below annotation with source range as 35.194.8.213 to allow only request from IP address - 35.194.8.213 to access our service.

    nginx.ingress.kubernetes.io/whitelist-source-range: "35.194.8.213"

We have created a new file "kube-backend-ingress-whitelist-nginx.yaml" which contains the added annotation.

```
apiVersion: extensions/v1beta1
kind: Ingress
metadata:
 name: kube-ingress-nginx
 annotations:
  kubernetes.io/ingress.class: nginx
  nginx.ingress.kubernetes.io/ssl-redirect: "false"
  nginx.ingress.kubernetes.io/whitelist-source-range: "35.194.8.213"
spec:
 rules:
 - http:
    paths:
    - backend:
        serviceName: kube-node-service-nginx
        servicePort: 8081
```

- o Before running the new configuration, delete the existing kube-ngress-nginx ingress (by selecting it and clicking delete from the Services & Ingress page). Run the following command to create Ingress.

  > kubectl apply -f kube-backend-ingress-whitelist-nginx.yaml

- o Test the microservice again by invoking the URL and you should see a 403 Forbidden error being printed on the console. This tests out the whitelisting for our ingress.

```
> curl -i http://35.231.11.11:80/fetchWebsite?key=AIzaSyC0m7d4cc-
jOwJIzymv9ntObF1ukIMr-Tc
```

Figure 41: 403 Forbidden Error

```
HTTP/1.1 403 Forbidden
Server: nginx/1.15.10
Date: Thu, 04 Jul 2019 04:22:22 GMT
Content-Type: text/html
Content-Length: 154
Connection: keep-alive

<html>
<head><title>403 Forbidden</title></head>
<body>
<center><h1>403 Forbidden</h1></center>
<hr><center>nginx/1.15.10</center>
</body>
</html>
```

We don't need to use Cloud Armor with Nginx Ingress as Nginx Ingress controller provides whitelisting and many features out of the box. This completes our production step.

Monitoring the Servers

Once the microservices are running, you can monitor the production environment by inspecting the logs at various entry points. All the logs are available in the Stack driver Console (Stack Driver -> Logging -> Log Viewer), and you can filter specific logs by selecting the corresponding components from drop down. For instance, in the example below, I have selected logs for api.naveenbalani.dev endpoints for a given time duration.

Figure 42: Endpoint logs in Stackdriver

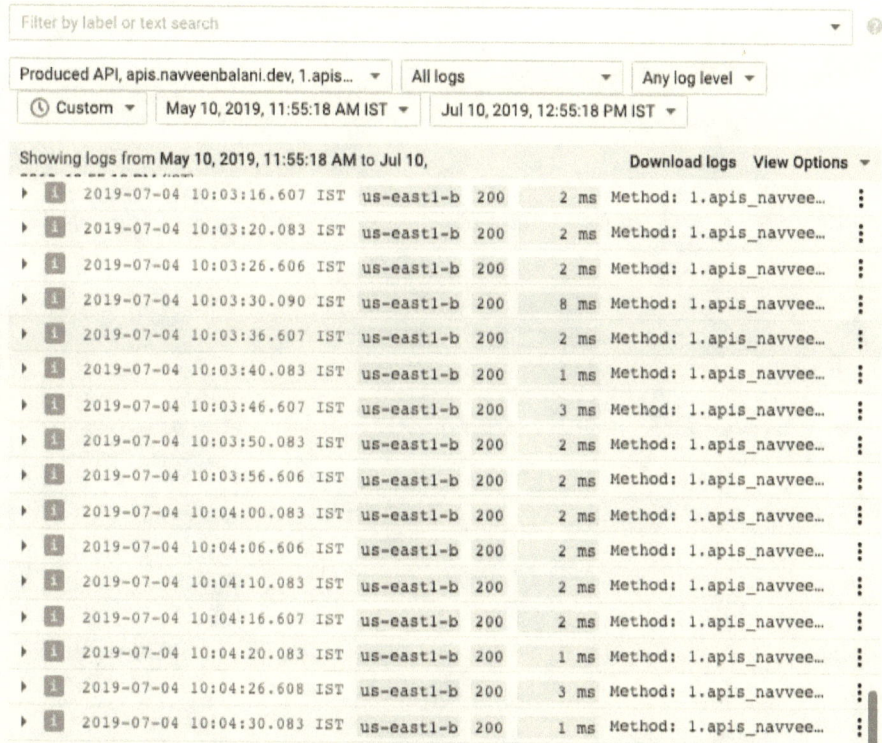

The following are a useful set of entry points for our application.

- Using Cloud Armor - This is the entry point to our environment, and when using Cloud Armor, we log every incoming request. You can view the complete incoming request in the stack driver console as described earlier.

- To monitor endpoints, you can visit Endpoint - > Service and you should see various details about the endpoint, such as request size, latency, error for each of the APIs as shown below.

Figure 43: Google Endpoint Console

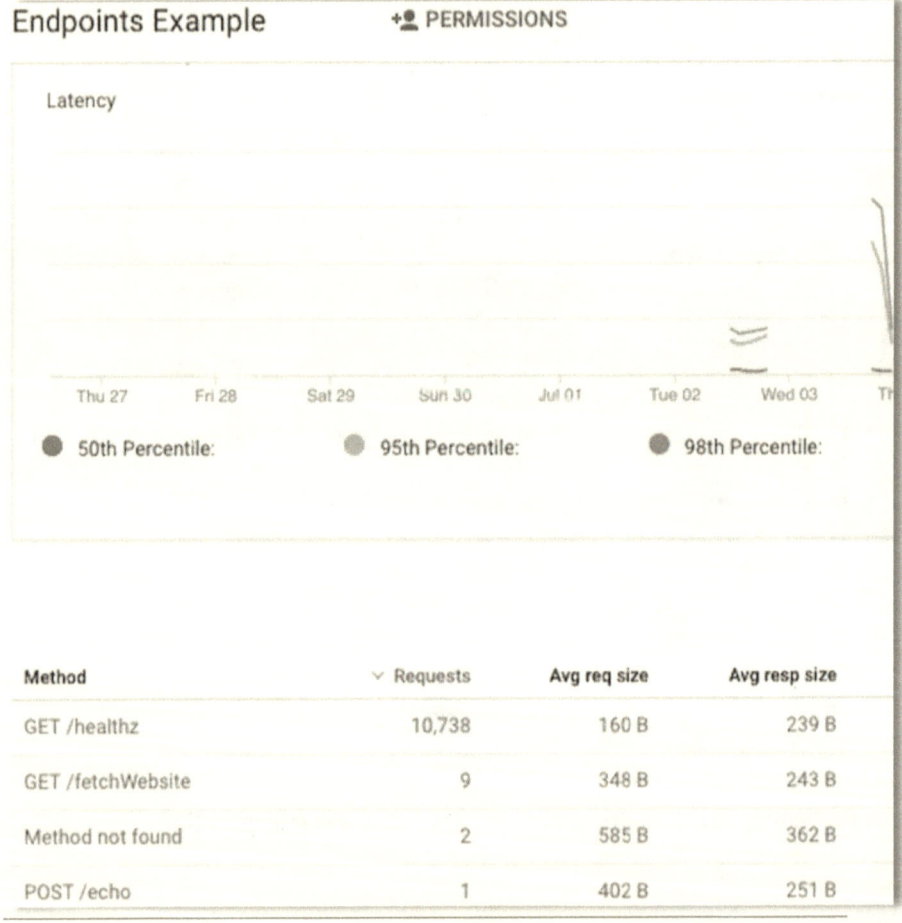

- Kubernetes Cluster Logs - All logs can be monitored through Stackdriver console by selecting Kubernetes - > <Region> -> <Kubernetes Cluster Name>. Kubernetes does not log your application logs. For your application logs, you can employ a sidecar logging agent (like fluentd) in your kubernetes cluster which streams our application logs to stackdriver. For more details, refer to this link- https://kubernetes.io/docs/concepts/cluster-administration/logging/#using-a-sidecar-container-with-the-logging-agent.

What's Next

The setup created in the book provides a reasonable production ready environment. However, you can harden the environment further by following the recommendations below:

- Each Google Kubernetes Engine node is given broad access by default (i.e. Compute Engine default service account) which has more permissions than required. You should create a minimally privileged service account to run your kubernetes cluster and add the required roles based on your application. For more details, refer to https://cloud.google.com/kubernetes-engine/docs/how-to/hardening-your-cluster#use_least_privilege_sa.

- If you use third-party containers and require only trusted container images be deployed on Google Kubernetes Engine (GKE), you can use a Binary Authorization service. For more details, refer to. https://cloud.google.com/binary-authorization/

- Define the appropriate Network Policy based on your application requirements. For instance, if you like to ensure only specific nodes in the pod can access the public network or specific IPs, and you can employ Network Policy resource on the cluster. For more details, refer to https://kubernetes.io/docs/concepts/services-networking/network-policies/.

Summary

In this book, we provided a detailed step by step introduction to setup a production-ready environment on Google Cloud. We went through setting up a private kubernetes cluster and deployed our microservices application on it.

We then created two Ingress Controllers – GCE and Nginx and went through the installation and configuration to expose our microservices over HTTPS protocol. We enabled NAT and whitelisting for our environment.

We touched upon how to monitor the environment and looked at various entry points for our application.

The steps outlined in the book were specific to Google Cloud, but similar configurations exist in all major cloud vendors like AWS and Azure.

In order to streamline load balancing, security configurations and setup across multiple cloud vendors, there are projects like Istio (https://istio.io/

) which provide service mesh like functionality for your environment. The next revision of the book would include how to use Istio configuration for our microservices application.

Dear Readers, Thank you for Reading.

We hope you enjoyed reading the book, and the information provided would be a valuable resource in designing and deploying production-ready microservices on google cloud.

As an author, we strive for comments and feedback to improve our book and would greatly appreciate if you could leave your valuable feedback.

Thank you.

www.ingramcontent.com/pod-product-compliance
Lightning Source LLC
Chambersburg PA
CBHW030018190526
45157CB00016B/3116